The
Gift
of
Thought

THE GIFT OF THOUGHT

WRITTEN AND ILLUSTRATED BY NIKI DEAN

Matador
9 Priory Business Park,
Wistow Road, Kibworth Beauchamp,
Leicestershire. LE8 0RX
Tel: 0116 279 2299
Email: books@troubador.co.uk
Web: www.troubador.co.uk/matador
Twitter: @matadorbooks

ISBN 978 1800461 932

British Library Cataloguing in Publication Data.
A catalogue record for this book is available from the British Library.

Printed and bound by CPI Group (UK) Ltd, Croydon, CR0 4YY
Typeset in 18pt Glacial Indifference by Troubador Publishing Ltd, Leicester, UK

Matador is an imprint of Troubador Publishing Ltd

MIX
Paper from
responsible sources
FSC® C013604
www.fsc.org

To Meg, Osc and Phe –
that you may discover a
world of peace and possibility...

I used to think my mind worked like a camera.

Snapping pictures of the world
around me. As it really is.

Storing them away as memories for when I need them again.

But sometimes, when other people look at the same things as me, they see them differently...

Cute

Love

TERRIFYING

HATE

Sometimes I feel differently about the same thing at different times. Like when I look at myself in the mirror...

Attractive

UGLY

Enough

NOT ENOUGH

Slim

FAT

I often have a lot of thoughts flying around inside my head.

About things...

...people, & situations

They burst in
and whizz around
really fast...

...or float in
and then float
away again.

But some of them get

STUCK

Those ones seem impossible to get rid of.

I can't shake them off.

I can't replace them
with better ones.

HSADpy

I can't pretend they aren't there.

Sometimes they even escalate!

Then my mind w a n d e r s . . .

...or a new thought just comes into my head.

And my outlook on life changes.

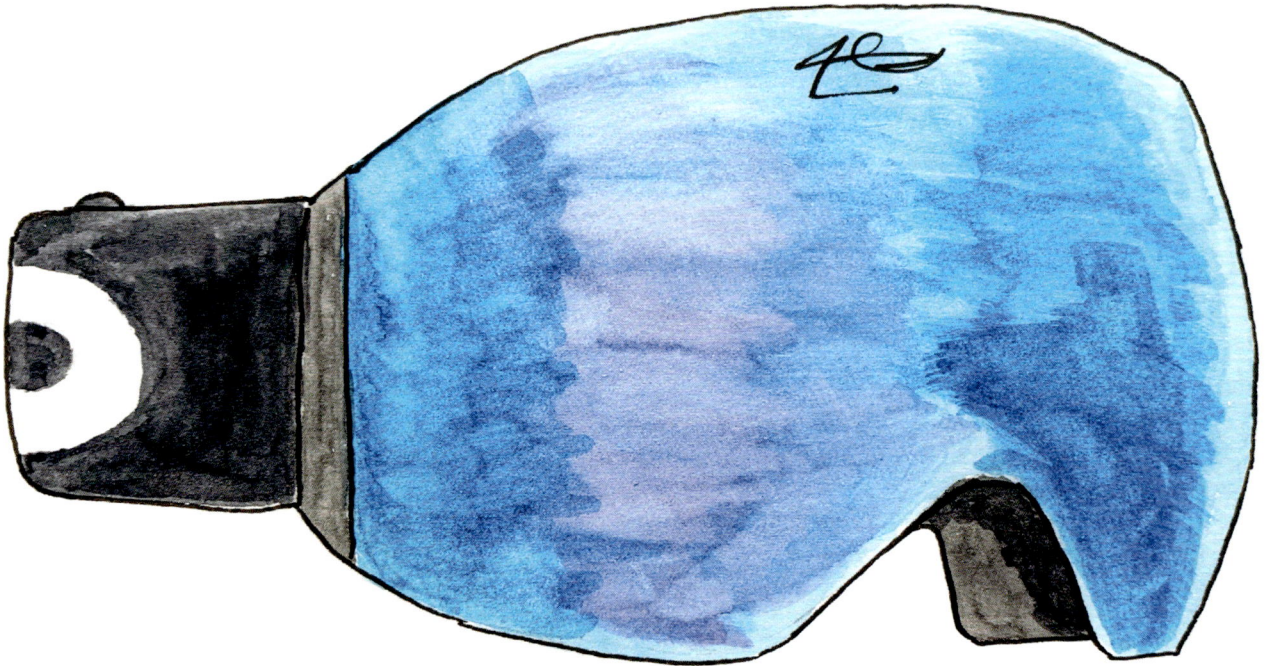

There definitely is a world out there.

Full of people. And places. And situations.

Where things happen.

Sometimes

good.

SOMETIMES

BAD.

But my experience of it all is created by Thought.

In truth, the world really comes to life in my head.

I'M THE MOVIE MAKER.

DIRECTOR

The script writer.

script

I EVEN HAVE

THE STARRING ROLE.

Thought is a gift we use to create anything and everything.

Without even realising it.

Sometimes I get...

ANXIOUS

ANGRY

Scared

...and I forget it's Thought.

Then I remember.

And I know there's nothing
I need to do about it...

I forget...

...then remember.

Forget. Remember.

Either way, I know I'm always safe.

It's all made of thought.

And it's all ok.

Matador